Madness & Other Colours

A Mythras Adventure
Written By Lawrence Whitaker

Editing
Alexandra James

Design and Layout
The Design Mechanism

Artist
Sarah Evans

Special Thanks
This scenario was written originally for the Stormbringer roleplaying game, published by Chaosium Inc, and first appeared in print in 'Ye Book of Tentacles vol. V', produced by Tentacles Press in 2003.
Our thanks goes to Fabian Küchler and Sarah Evans for their help in bringing this version of the scenario to Mythras.

Find Us At
www.thedesignmechanism.com and www.mythrasrpg.com.
Facebook: https://www.facebook.com/The-Design-Mechanism
G+: https://plus.google.com/communities/113034383032729983266

Mythras is a trademark of The Design Mechanism. All rights reserved. This edition of Madness & Other Colours is copyright © 2016. This book may not be reproduced in whole or in part by any means without permission from The Design Mechanism, except as quoted for purposes of illustration, discussion, and game play. Reproduction of the material in this book for the purposes of personal or corporate profit, by photographic, electronic, or other methods of retrieval is strictly prohibited.

For details of the Mythras Gateway license, please contact The Design Mechanism
(designmechanism@gmail.com).

Published under license in the UK by Aeon Games Publishing
www.aeongamespublishing.co.uk
ISBN 978-1-91147-122-6

Printed in Great Britain

For a free PDF of this item please contact
office@aeongamespublishing.co.uk with proof of purchase

Madness & Other Colours

Madness & Other Colours involves the characters in the bickering between two art collectors, eventually leading to a hazardous trip to the island of a long-dead sorcerer and a confrontation with the sorcerer's imprisoned spirit. The scenario begins in any large town or city capable of supporting artists and their patrons, but moves to the island in question for the latter part of the action. Games Masters can, if they wish, change the island to a remote, inland destination, just as long as the location is isolated from civilisation. Some suggestions for placing and using the scenario are as follows:

Meeros

The city could be Meeros itself or even Tithys, described in the scenario *Xamoxis' Cleansing*. Loric Nygh was a sorcerer serving the Badoshi Warlord known as Sool the Mighty (founder of the city of E'kn), and his stronghold is on one of the many small islands lying south of Meeros.

The Realm

Nor Port, West Port or Cylder are perfect for the city. Loric Nygh was a sorcerer from the time of Sayalis and his fight against the Chaos Mother, with the Emperor Sool the Mighty ruling over the Twin Lakes area of The Realm. The stronghold is located on a remote island somewhere off the west coast.

Thennla

Borissa is the city, Emperor Sool was a petty warmonger with delusions of grandeur from before the Cataclysm, and Loric Nygh was an Assabian sorcerer-mercenary. There are countless islands off the coast of Korantia and Methalea where Nygh formed his stronghold.

Scourged Earth & Monster Island

The *Mythras Games Masters' Pack* outlines the Scourged Earth setting which is perfect for this scenario. Games Masters will need to create a city and island, but there are many in the Scourged Earth. Alternatively, Monster Island makes a perfect home for the Ciirt, Maligaunt and Loric Nygh.

Serjedny & Baldomeer

The City or Town where this story begins is home to several wealthy collectors of artworks. Fashions amongst them come and go like the trade winds that batter the nearby harbour. Currently the vogue is for rare sculptures of the kind produced during the reign of Emperor Sool the 3rd (or some other despotic ruler who had plenty of tame sorcerers), Supreme Ruler of the Soolian Empire approximately two thousand years ago. It was Sool's habit of having his enemies cast alive into bronze statuettes and then sorcerously shrunk to a manageable size for subsequent display.

Serjedny The Immaculate and *Baldomeer The Vain* are collectors of art and bitter rivals. Their feud is long-running and driven by mutual obsession. If one makes a rare acquisition, then the other goes to elaborate extremes to better it. As their obsession grows, so does their antagonism. Baldomeer has seemingly acquired one of the Sool Statuettes. Around eight inches in height, the statuette represents a young woman, naked save for the wrapping of her extraordinarily long hair. Baldomeer claims that the statue weeps tears of molten bronze, which guarantees its authenticity. Since the Sool statuettes are currently much sought after, Baldomeer intends to flaunt his acquisition at a public unveiling of the item. Serjedny, incandescent with jealousy, means to disrupt his rival's success. To do this, he wants to expose the statuette as a fake, thereby discrediting his enemy. Second, he wants to procure the statuette for himself; fake or not, it will make a fitting trophy for his enemy's downfall.

A Tear in Bronze

The statuette is very real and very powerful. The person represented is Mistress Krystya, concubine to Emperor Sool. She made the mistake of enjoying a dalliance with Lord Sleane, one of Sool's trusted advisers. Mistress Krystya was ritually dismembered, the remains of her still-living body then cast in marble and bronze, and her soul sealed into the statuette. Sleane suffered a worse fate: flayed, salted, quartered and trepanated, his own soul was then cast into Krystya's bronze prison. These two souls reside within the cast, writhing still in the pain of their torture, and unable to escape the torment. All they seek is a merciful release; but as the centuries of interminable pain have twisted their desires, they have constructed the joint power to manipulate others through the fabric of the statuette.

The lovers were imprisoned by Sool's most powerful sorcerer, *Loric Nygh*. Only Loric Nygh has the power to release the trapped souls through a certain device. This device is found in only one place – Nygh's stronghold – and is one of the feared *Entropy Configurators*. Whoever possesses the statuette is compelled to take it to Nygh's lair and seek-out the Configurator, resorting to whatever means necessary to complete the journey. Once in the thrall of the statuette, madness is the inevitable result, and with it comes an all-too real sample of the pain experienced by the entrapped lovers. It takes an enormous effort of will to free oneself of the statuette's spell; suicide tends to be the only effective way.

The statuette's influence is subtle and requires several days to take hold. First, the dreams of the whoever possesses the statuette are dominated by erotic thoughts involving Mistress Krystya. Upon waking, the dreamer is afflicted with a mournful sadness and, as the dreams progress, develops an insistent longing to bring solace to the beautiful, wronged, concubine. After several such dreams, the images change to those of the wrathful adviser to Emperor Sool. These are violent, vengeful dreams, and upon waking the dreamer possesses a furious hatred of anyone who might stand in their way. Together, and over a period of about a week, the owner of the statuette becomes insular, obsessive and prone to outbursts of verbal and physical violence. By the beginning of the second week, a desire to seek-out Nygh's Stronghold develops, and this desire consumes every waking moment. If these thoughts are shoved aside, or distractions sought, the individual suffers excruciating pain, as though their flesh has been flayed from their body and salt rubbed into the wounds. Only by returning one's thoughts to travelling to Nygh's Stronghold is the pain assuaged. By the beginning of the third week, the desire to reach Nygh's Stronghold is dominant, and, driven by the restless souls of the statuette, the owner undertakes the journey, regardless of risk. By the end of the eighth week, madness results and the owner of the statue, sensing the futility of the quest, either loses their mind completely (becoming a gibbering wreck) or commits suicide. The statuette is then abandoned and awaits the next servant.

This descent into madness is abstracted through the development of a Passion: *Release the Lovers*. It begins at a value equal to 100 minus the character's Willpower, and grows at a rate of 2d6% each week until it reaches (or exceeds) 100%, indicating complete insanity. The character can attempt to battle the urges of the Passion through opposed Willpower rolls, but each time a Willpower roll fails to beat the Passion, the next (and subsequent) rolls are at a further level of difficulty.

Beginning the Scenario

The characters are acquaintances of Serjedny The Immaculate. Perhaps they have worked for him before, procuring rare treasures, or have been introduced to him as professional adventurers who could work for him in the future. Whatever the reason, they have been invited to a meal at Serjedny's opulent home overlooking the Great Market.

"Several Sool statuettes have been found over the past years," Serjedny says between mouthfuls of food, "and every single one has proved to be a forgery. What makes Baldomeer so arrogant as to believe he has the real thing? All the Sool Statuettes have been destroyed or lost. Baldomeer lies. And he does so to provoke me! His lies are so plausible that I am becoming a laughing stock. Baldomeer will pay! The bastard shall *rue* the day!" And he waves his fork around in the air, as though wielding a rapier, to make the point.

Serjedny's outburst continues for over an hour. "Of course, his trickery must be exposed. Baldomeer claims the statuette cries tears of molten bronze! If only I could get to the statuette before he unveils it and show it does not! Come the day of the unveiling he would be exposed as the charlatan he is."

The characters applaud the idea, especially as Serjedny offers 1000 Silver for their help, or the equivalent in artworks from his collection.

Testing, Testing

Serjedny knows that more conclusive proof of the statuette's veracity is required than whether or not it weeps bronze tears – a simple cantrip could provide tears easily enough. Serjedny knows from his research that the bronze used in the casting of the Sool Statuettes reacts in a particular way with certain reagents. Serjedny provides the characters with a vial containing the chemical concoction: three droplets need to be applied to the surface of the statuette; if it is genuine, a small, blue mark will be left on the bronze. If it is a fake, then the bronze will be unaffected.

Of course Baldomeer knows the same technique and has already used it, proving the statuette to be genuine. Serjedny needs to be certain that what he believes is true: if the statuette is fake, the characters can leave it there, and Serjedny will expose the fraud in due course. But, if it is real – which Serjedny highly doubts – then the characters should steal it, for it is of incredible value.

To test the statuette, the characters need to gain access to Baldomeer's house. The location is well-known, and usually Baldomeer retains a vigilant hired guard. However Serjedny notes that recently, most of Baldomeer's staff have been dismissed: "Further proof of his trickery! If he possesses the genuine article, why dismiss those who need to guard it? Baldomeer has a fake and knows his ruination is imminent. Why, he can no longer afford to pay guards and servants any longer!"

It is true that Baldomeer has dismissed his staff, but this is due to the nature of the madness that has afflicted him, and has nothing to do with the imminent downfall at Serjedny's hands.

Baldomeer's Home

Baldomeer's home is in the hills north of the city. Set in its own grounds and hidden from view by thick, untidy bushes and shrubs, it is a single-storey villa of a typical style. The wall surrounding the villa is three metres high and topped with spikes. A winding gravel driveway leads to the main entrance, continuing around to the stables where seven fine horses are housed.

During their attempt to locate and test the statuette, the characters are likely to encounter Baldomeer. He can be found anywhere in the villa, but most likely in his room, or drunk in the wine cellar. Far from being angered at their trespass on his property, he welcomes

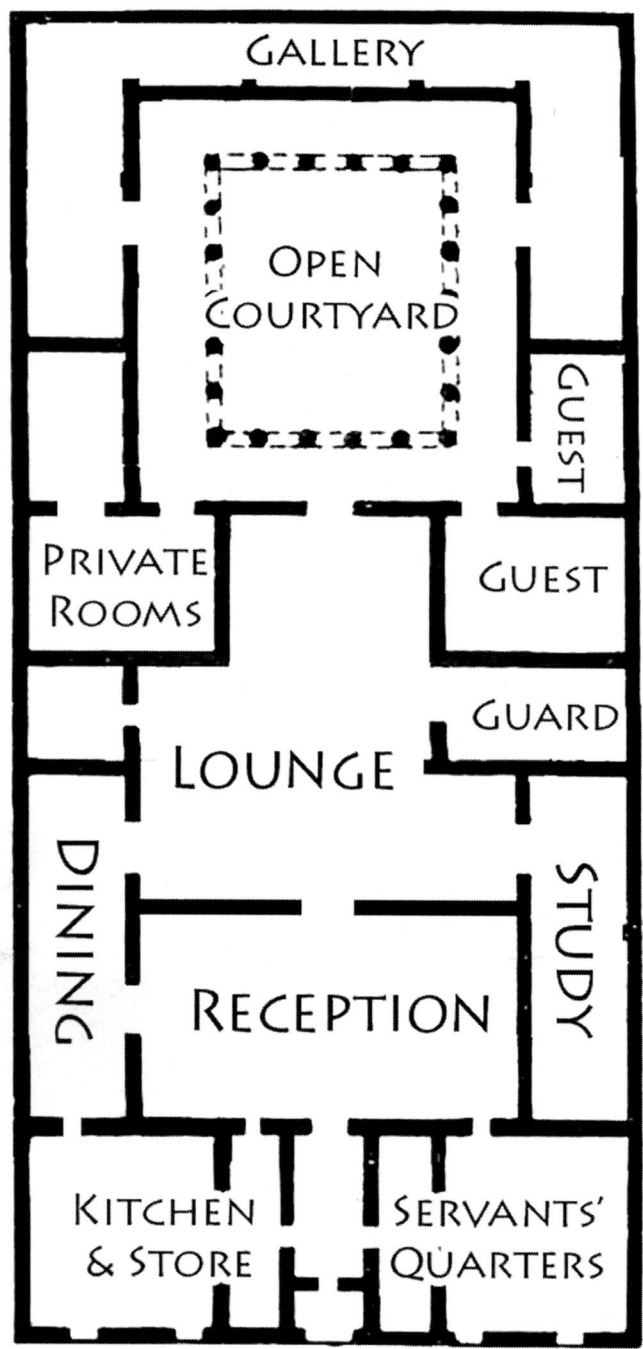

Reception

The front door opens into this exquisitely appointed reception area. Superb furniture and expensive tapestries and artworks decorate the area, as one might expect of someone who collects art for a living.

Study

Baldomeer's study is a wood-panelled and book/scroll-lined room, musty with the scent of ancient, moldering knowledge. Most of the texts found here cover art and its history; a hundred different periods and a thousand different subjects. Should any of the characters decide to look for information on the Sool Statuettes, they find themselves in for a long search. A successful Perception roll is needed, and 2d4 hours in which to undertake it. Once they find the ancient, crumbling scroll, there is little information to be had; nothing more than a little history about Sool and a few scant descriptions of some of the statuettes.

Lounge

Lovingly furnished in a manner similar to the reception area. There are many things of value in here, but most too large to steal easily.

Dining Room

Dominated by an ebony and marble table that can easily seat twenty people. Rich tapestries line the east wall whilst the west contains a full length and height mosaic depicting the a great historical battle, in all its chaos and gore.

Kitchen and Store

A well stocked and ordered kitchen and store area. Food has been scattered carelessly around, much of it half-eaten – an indication of the increasing madness Baldomeer suffers. Across one wall, Baldomeer has daubed some words in what appears to be blood (but is, in fact, raspberry jam). The words read: *Nygh's Island! Free Them! Free Them!* In the north west corner of the kitchen is a trapdoor, easily lifted, that reveals steps leading down to the cellar.

Cellar (Beneath Kitchen)

Accessed via narrow stairs in the kitchen, the cellar runs the full width of the house, and beneath the the kitchen, servants' quarters and reception. Racks line the walls and several large casks sit in one corner. Like the kitchen, empty bottles and urns are scattered across the stone flags of the floor where Baldomeer has drunk himself into a stupor in order to dull the pain he experiences.

Guard Room

Before Baldomeer began to lose his senses, his two bodyguards slept here. Both the room and its bunk beds are empty, the blankets dumped in a heap on the floor.

Guest Rooms

Each is sumptuously furnished, although they have been unused for quite some time.

Servants' Quarters

Again, unoccupied, since Baldomeer dismissed his servants some time ago.

the chance to open his tortured soul to them. In a long, rambling monologue, he tells them of how imperative it is to venture to Nygh's Stronghold and deliver the statuette to 'The Machine' – only then can all of them be saved. He offers money, status and power – all of which are within his abilities to provide – and throughout his speech, he remains utterly convincing.

Baldomeer once employed several guards to protect his property, but since the madness brought by the statuette has ensnared him, he has dismissed them all, fearing they may try to steal his treasure. At this stage, all he wants is to be alone with the statuette, although he yearns already for Nygh's Stronghold.

Private Rooms

Baldomeer's private rooms, leading into a sunken bathing area. Again, expensive furnishings crowd the room, but most are too large to liberate easily. Baldomeer is likely to be found here, wracked with pain and delusion, squirming naked on his huge, silk-swathed bed. Aside from the huge bed, there are several large trunks packed with expensive clothes for all manner of weathers and occasions, including a bronze cuirass and kilt (AP6, Chest and Abdomen) suitable for someone of SIZ 11 or 12.

Gallery

Here are Baldomeer's most precious works: paintings, statues, pottery, and so on, displayed reverentially on marble and obsidian plinths. There are over fifty exhibits, ranging from ancient and rare (a dragon saddle, for instance), to relatively recent works. It is impossible to calculate the wealth contained in here, but what the characters seek can be found tucked away in one corner; the Sool Statuette. The statuette is unremarkable. A piece of marble and bronze, 24cm in height, and green with age. It represents a naked woman of immense beauty, her modesty wreathed in her long, flowing hair. The face of the statuette is pained, as though wracked with great suffering. And, every minute or so, a tear of liquid bronze dribbles from one of the eyes and sizzles on the marble of the plinth. Touching the statuette creates no strange sensations and presents little danger: prolonged possession (1d3 days) is needed for the Passion to take effect.

Baldomeer's Pain

Baldomeer has had the Sool Statuette for four weeks. His life is now a misery. His dreams are filled with images of violent death coupled with unbridled lust, and his waking hours are consumed by the desire to find Nygh's Stronghold and deliver the statuette to its final destination: the Entropy Configurator, or The Machine, as he names it. He has tried to concentrate on other tasks, but is gripped by intense pain whenever he does so. He has resolved to make the journey to Nygh's Stronghold and intends to announce this plan at the unveiling of the statuette, in the hope that stating his intentions to the world will ease his suffering. Bordering on insanity, Baldomeer cares nothing for Serjedny's schemes: reaching Nygh's Stronghold is all that matters. He does know that he needs help; the journey will be hazardous, and he requires bodyguards – more for the statuette than his own, miserable life. He is willing to pay handsomely for any company he can acquire, and this means the characters. If the characters require such persuasion, he can easily offer each of them 600 Silver, with a similar bonus once the statuette has been delivered to The Machine.

Another option, which Baldomeer only considers if it is suggested to him, is for the characters to perhaps relieve him of the burden and take the statuette on his behalf (whether or not they intend simply giving it to Serjedny). A Formidable Deceit or Influence roll is required to convince Baldomeer of the wisdom of this, opposed by Baldomeer's Release the Lovers 84%. It would relieve him of the madness and despair, but he would not wish this pain even on Serjedny and he continually voices his reluctance even if he eventually agrees.

Options for the Characters

Help Baldomeer

This poor wretch needs help in getting to Nygh's Stronghold. The Release the Lovers Passion provides instinctive direction to whoever it inflicts and whoever holds the statue. Therefore Baldomeer, at least, can provide a route to wherever Nygh's Stronghold is located.

Continue with the Plan

Testing the statuette proves to be easy. If the characters keep the statuette, whoever is in charge of it suffers the same fate as Baldomeer. If handed to Serjedny, he suffers – and eventually pleads with the characters to take him to Nygh's Stronghold.

Do Nothing

The unveiling goes as planned. Held in the grounds of Baldomeer's home, a large and influential crowd has gathered, the characters and Serjedny among them. Baldomeer appears, after an extremely long wait (which annoys the guests but delights Serjedny) and refuses to unveil the statuette, which he carries, wrapped in a crimson cloth of silk. He rambles at interminable length about the tragedy that befalls lovers and how solace can be found only at Nygh's Stronghold. He pleads for someone to help him in his quest, provoking cruel laughter and a barrage of insults (mostly orchestrated by Serjedny). Close to breaking point, Baldomeer, still clutching his statuette, staggers indoors. If no one helps him, his body is discovered in the sunken bath several days later, his wrists slashed and the statuette, still wrapped in the cloth, beside his body. Serjedny steps forward to claim the statuette, claiming that Baldomeer's guilt over having faked such a valuable item clearly drove him to suicide. With the statuette now in his possession, Serjedny follows a similar fate to his dead rival.

The Island

The island where Loric Nygh built his stronghold is relatively flat. A crescent beach slopes steadily upwards to a forested or jungled plateau. Vegetation is dense and home to many different forms of wildlife, some of which are hostile and some of which are the results of Loric Nygh's gruesome experiments back when he was in physical command of the ecosystem. At the top of the foodchain are

Loric Nygh's Island

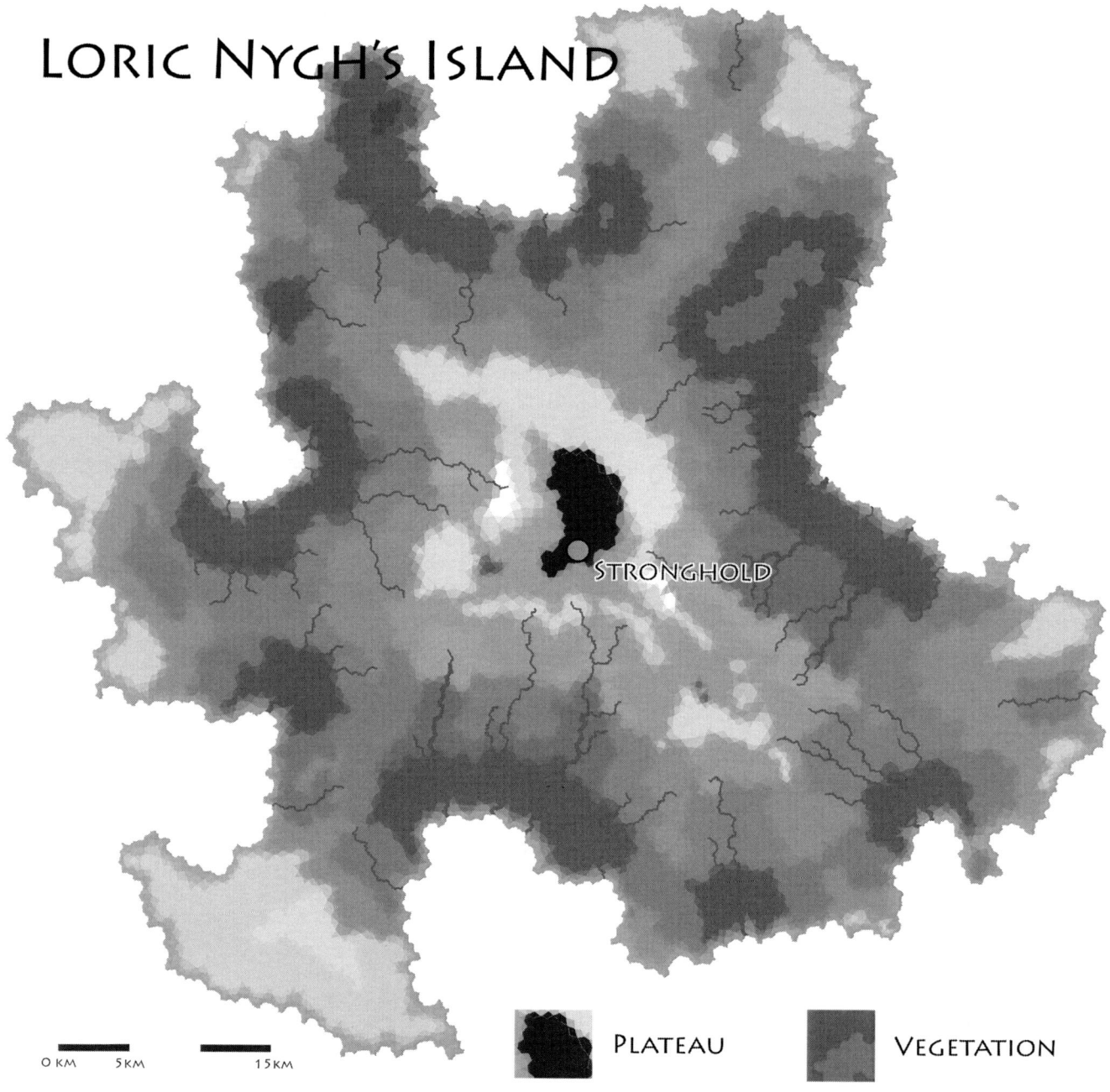

PLATEAU   VEGETATION

the Ciirt, primitive ab-humans that strayed here several centuries ago, and Maligaunt, Nygh's demon servant.

The Cirrt do not keep a vigilant watch on the beach and coastline; aside from the occasional ship that might pause to investigate, no one knows the Ciirt are here and intentional visitors simply do not occur. If they get the chance the Ciirt capture and eat errant sailors who pause by the island and venture into the interior, but usually the Ciirt ignore them.

This time, things are different. Both Maligaunt and Loric Nygh are sensitive to the psychic agony of the statuette and the moment someone touches shore carrying it, both are aware of its presence. The Ciirt are instructed to lure or bring the characters to the settlement, but not to harm them (for now). A small hunting party of 12 Ciirt are sent to watch the beach and monitor the characters' movements. The Ciirt's job is to ensure they move inland and, when the beach is far behind them, usher them onwards to the stronghold so they can be observed. Maligaunt has plans for the characters. Great plans. *Awful* plans.

The map of the island shows the relief and location of the stronghold. The Ciirt take approximately two hours from the characters' landing on the island to reach a place where they can observe movements. For several hours the Ciirt stay hidden, tracking and observing. Their Stealth rolls are Easy, representing their intimacy with the environment, while Perception rolls for the characters are at Hard, representing their lack of it. As the characters make their way through the undergrowth, they should be aware of *something* watching them, but until the Ciirt reveal themselves, they do not know what.

There is a 45% chance of two encounters while the characters slowly progress, rolled (1d6) or chosen from the following list:

> ### Sailing Fateful Seas
> *Few captains with any brains will sail to unknown or poorly charted islands simply because the characters want them to. However there is always some unscrupulous down-on-his-or-her-luck captain willing to make a perilous voyage if enough silver is offered. With some hunting around at the harbour, simulated by either a Streetwise or Hard Locale roll, Captain Ramin, a drink-soaked sea salt of the lowest order can be found. Desperate to pay a crew that has threatened to insert a telescope into a deeply personal orifice, Ramin can be persuaded with an Influence or Commerce roll to sail to Nygh's island for a sum of 500 Silver, which either of the art collectors can easily pay.*
>
> *Ramin's ship, The Dawn Piper, is a ramshackle, barely floating heap of barnacle-crusted timbers that should, by rights, be at the bottom of an ocean somewhere and infested with moray eels. Sadly it's here, available, and capable of getting the characters to the island more or less in one piece. The thing takes on water at roughly the same speed Captain Ramin takes on grog, and the all-too-mutinous crew spend all their time bailing water and precious little on other duties. Have each character make an Endurance roll for each day of the voyage. Failure results in either intense sea sickness for the day, flea bites, rat bites, or an infestation of lice in any available thatch of hair.*
>
> *Still, The Dawn Piper makes it to the island and Captain Ramin will wait for the characters to return to the ship when their mission is complete. Several of the crew may desert, and perhaps, if needed, one or two mikght accompany the characters into the island's interior, if paid at least 10 Silver for the job.*

1. Basilisk
2. Beetle, Giant
3. Flying Fire Ants Swarm
4. Maggots of Torment
5. Mantis, Giant
6. Snare

For creatures' statistics, see the Non-Players Character Statistics section beginning on page 16.

Basilisk (see Mythras, page 229)

Maligaunt hatched this monster from an experimental egg he found in Nygh's caverns. Realising what it was (he is immune to its gaze), he released it into the jungle and it now scratches out a meagre existence. The characters might be alerted to something being wrong by first coming across a petrified Ciirt hunter hidden in the undergrowth, a victim of the basilisk's stare. Otherwise the basilisk simply emerges from the vegetation, squawking and flapping its wings, head swinging around to stare at whatever has disturbed it.

Beetle, Giant (see Mythras page 230)

Grubbing around beneath a pile of decaying branches and leaves, all this beetle wants is to be left alone. The characters disturb it and it lashes out at the nearest character (roll randomly), biting at the ankles or legs (roll 1d10 for Hit Location, rather than 1d20) for no more than one round before hurriedly digging back underground.

Flying Fire Ants (see Mythras page 251)

A nest of flying fire ants is advertently disturbed, causing a SIZ 12 swarm of these stinging, winged insects. The swarm has 3 Action Points and inflicts 1d3 damage. The bites they leave actively burn – a result of digestive acids the ants produce – leaving nasty, hot welts that feel like the scald of a branding iron.

Maggots of Torment

Created by Loric Nygh, these are actually the warped enemies of the sorcerer that have been condemned to an eternity of misery until killed by violence. There are six maggots and they huddle together for companionship. Their sickly white bodies are 60 centimetres long and 30 centimetres thick. Their heads are vaguely human, with twisted, ancient features, half-blind, watery eyes, and gaping, toothless mouths. On detecting footfalls, they wriggle from their hiding place and towards the characters, mouths working silently, eyes pleading for mercy. The mercy they want is to be killed; their mouths are sounding the words for 'kill me' in ancient tongues (Insight rolls are needed to understand what they truly want). They jostle for the privilege of death, writhing over each other to get close to the nearest potential assailant. Their stench is revolting; Endurance rolls are needed to avoid feelings of nausea that make all skills while in their presence Hard.

The maggots have 3 Hit Points each and only a single Hit Location. They are easy to kill and welcome death, but killing a maggot triggers a Disruption spell bound into the wretch that affects its killer. See Mythras page 125 for details.

Mantis, Giant (see Mythras page 257)

Concealed in the branches of a tall (40 metres in height), leafy tree, this mantis strikes at the person bringing up the rear of the party. It's tactic is to strike, grab, and then retreat up into the canopy layer of the forest to devour its meal at leisure.

Snare

A very simple small game snare, this concealed length of hide is formed into a slip-noose with its longer end attached to a nearby tree stump. It requires a Herculean Perception roll to spot, and if a random character fails, it loops around an ankle, draws tight as the leg moves forward, constricts around the limb (inflicting 1d2 damage) and causes the victim to trip sharply, suffering a further 1d3 points of damage from the fall. The snare can be easily removed, but it does alert the characters to a an intelligent presence on the island.

Secrets of Nygh's Stronghold

Nygh's Stronghold, wherever it is located for the purposes of the adventure, is long ruined – as all good sorcerers' lairs should be. However, it is still occupied. The *Ciirt*, a race of stunted, bestial humanoids (which may be orcs or goblins, if preferred), migrated here several centuries ago and made Nygh's Stronghold their home. The Ciirt have changed little in their habits or appearance. Their intellect is limited, and their culture confined to subsistence farming, hunting and, when times are hard, the odd spot of cannibalism.

Yet they are not alone. Loric Nygh's Entropy Configurators still exist in the caverns beneath the stronghold. And, confined to the place of their creation, his ultimate creations, the *Walking Spells*, still wander aimlessly.

Following the events in the City, the characters are likely to find themselves travelling to Nygh's Stronghold, either bearing the statuette themselves, or accompanying either Serjedny or Baldomeer. If bearing the statuette, they experience the insanity it brings. The madness reaches its peak half-way through the journey, and begins to subside as Nygh's Stronghold draws closer. The trapped souls sense the proximity of their destination and relax their grip as freedom beckons. The sickening pain lifts noticeably, although the erotic dreams continue as Mistress Krystya rewards the statue bearer for their perserverance. If either Baldomeer or Serjedny carry the statue, the characters notice a marked change in their behaviour. The mood swings become less, and their constant moans of pain turn to barely whimpers (and sometimes whimpers of pleasure).

Eventually Nygh's Stronghold looms from the dense mists or forest/jungle surrounding it. A spiky crown of land surrounded by jagged cliffs of granite appears. The characters become aware of a constant whispering on the air – a thousand muted tongues chattering quietly in some ancient language. This place is still and forbidding, but it could almost be surrounded by the displaced souls of those who died at the hand of Loric Nygh's vile magics.

The map on page 6 shows the major features of Nygh's Island.

The Rise and Demise of Loric Nygh

Loric Nygh rose to prominence under the rule of Emperor Sool 3rd (known also as the Shining Emperor, Sool the Mighty, Sool the Stupid or Sool the Who? depending on whom is consulted). Always an exceptional scholar of sorcery, Loric Nygh's talents were recognised and indulged early-on by Sool, and he was quickly made the key architect of the Shining Emperor's plans for his Empire.

A dutiful student of magic, and worshipper of vile, blasphemous gods, Loric Nygh's abiding interest was in the nature of magic itself, and his studies led him to discover the true fabric of reality and the many dimensions where demons and other things of the supernatural dwell. In order to perfect his knowledge, Loric Nygh retired to his stronghold and began the construction of his Entropy Configurators. Sool, his emperor and patron, visited often, bringing with him those he wanted punished. Loric Nygh built the Forge and Sculptor solely to please Sool, and the Shining Emperor was so pleased with these new means of torture that he granted Loric Nygh free rein in his experiments.

Through his discoveries of hidden worlds, Loric Nygh learned how to steal magic. He stole from many mortal sorcerers and spirits, but made the mistake of stealing magic from gods or powerful demons. Eventually, they took their revenge and, forming a hideous army, assaulted Nygh's Stronghold. Nygh could do little against such powerful beings and was soon overwhelmed. His body was broken over many days, using the same machines that he had used to break Sool's enemies. Then, ripping his soul from what remained of his carcass, the Elder Beings, their scourging finished, imprisoned Nygh's spirit in one of his own devices, there to remain for eternity, pain-wracked but sapient, a prisoner of ambition and forced to watch the aeons come and go. Nygh's soul remains, and yearns for release.

As Gods Are

Trapped in one of his own infernal machines, Loric Nygh craves a suitable host for his huge, hideous intellect. The Ciirt are simply unworthy; their brains are not developed enough to accommodate the weight of his knowledge and power. A few souls over the centuries have been tested and have failed. With the arrival of the characters, Loric Nygh could have a suitable vessel allowing him to once more dominate the world and take revenge on the Elder Beings who destroyed him. Loric Nygh likens himself to a god, and believes that, if he does what a god does often enough, he will become as gods are. The success of this plan hinges utterly on how the characters handle their encounter with the entrapped soul of Loric Nygh.

Ciirt

Upon reaching the Ciirt settlement, the characters are made welcome by these strange, bestial folk. The reception is neither ostentatious nor threatening. Food is provided, shelter loaned and some basic comforts offered. Ciirt cuisine is disgusting to human palettes; rotten meat and fish is highly prized, and drenched in a pungent and sickening sauce of decayed vegetation. The Ciirt care little if the characters eat; they have been instructed to welcome the characters by Loric Nygh's servant, the demon Maligaunt.

Maligaunt

The last of Nygh's faithful servants, Maligaunt hid from the army that exacted justice, two thousand years ago, but has remained close to the Stronghold, trying to offer succour to Nygh's imprisoned spirit. Maligaunt acts as the focus for the Ciirt's worship, conducting made-up rituals that seek to reinforce Nygh's insistence that he is becoming a god. It is Maligaunt's task to find a suitable host for his master's soul, and he spends an entire day watching the characters before revealing himself.

Maligaunt is tall and spindle-thin. His head is almost bald, save for a few whisps of pale hair that flutter behind his scalp whether a breeze exists or not. His face borders on the skeletal, and his eyes shine with a golden light. As demons go, he is human enough to gaze upon, but he possesses incredible strength and reflexes, making him a fearsome opponent in combat. After observing the characters, he selects the one with the highest POW to be the recipient of Loric Nygh's soul. His approach is subtle. He reveals himself shortly before the meal offered to the characters on the morning after their arrival on Nygh's Stronghold. He listens to their story about the statuette, nodding sagely, and then, after some deliberation, announces that he knows precisely of a machine that will free the tortured souls of Mistress Krystya and Lord Sleane; indeed, he can recount the story of their torture and transformation with much relish, almost as though he was there (which, of course, he was, as Formidable Insight rolls may reveal). But such kindness comes at a price. To trigger the spell required to free the lovers, the character with the highest POW must sacrifice some of their own magical energy to give freedom to the entombed lovers. "Not a lot, you understand," Maligaunt assures them. "A mild disorientation will result but should pass within a few hours." Whoever is inflicted with the Release the Lovers Passion sides with Maligaunt – even if this is the character with the highest POW, such is the desire to see Krystya and Sleane freed.

Maligaunt's plan is simple. One of the characters is placed in the reception chamber of the machine holding Loric Nygh's soul. Loric Nygh takes possession of the character's body and he is rampant once more, the character's soul trapped in place of Nygh's. Nygh holds good on Maligaunt's promise to free the trapped souls in the Statuette; they are placed in the Sculptor, a separate machine, but are subject to a horribly grim joke as a result (see the description of The Sculptor later in the scenario).

Options for the Characters

Below are how some likely actions by the characters are handled by Maligaunt and the Ciirt

- **Maligaunt's deal declined.** With a deep sigh of regret, Maligaunt states that the souls in the statuette can never be free unless one of the characters is prepared to make the small sacrifice he has suggested. But, if the characters are so reluctant, then they should be prepared for the torment of the statuette to become worse, now that they are so close to the final goal and are denying the lovers release. He begs them to reconsider. If they do not, he and the Ciirt employ force to overwhelm the party. If caught, the character with the highest POW is sacrificed to Loric Nygh whilst the others are sacrificed to the hideous Walking Spells.
- **Characters Use Force.** Using force to get Maligaunt to co-operate is met with much heavier force. Both Maligaunt and the Ciirt fight to kill the characters, although sparing the one with the highest POW. This adventurer is then sacrificed to Loric Nygh.
- **Characters Flee.** Maligaunt and the Ciirt pursue them in a ritualised Hunt, complete with horns and hounds the Ciirt keep for hunting small game. If caught, the adventurer with the highest POW is sacrificed to Loric Nygh whilst the others are sacrificed to the Walking Spells.

The Ciirt Settlement

The Ciirt have made their home in the ruins of Loric Nygh's palace. Little is left of the building, but even to an untrained eye, this was once an immense and labyrinthine structure. As the characters approach the clearing where the settlement lurks, the Ciirt make themselves visible, folding out of the thinning undergrowth and emerging from their shabby settlements of mud, hide and dung. There are four hundred Ciirt, with children of both sexes accounting for half the population. Old-aged Ciirt are few. They are generally

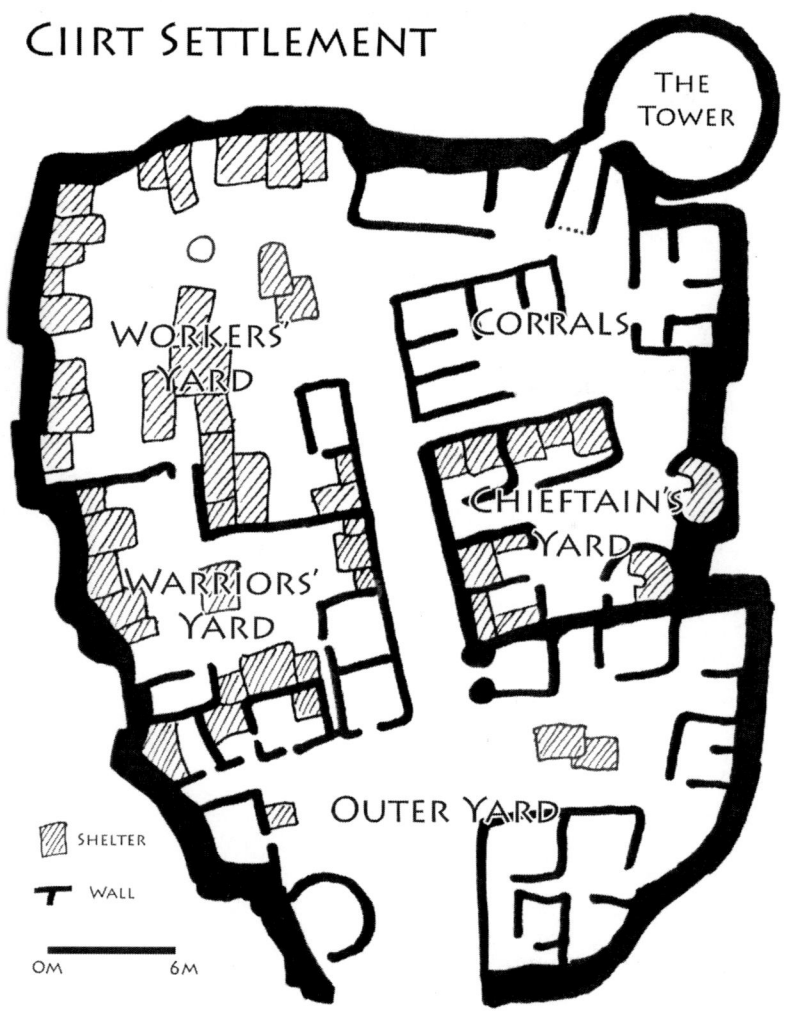

eaten by the younger members of the community when they can no longer hunt, bear children or make themselves useful. Of the adult Ciirt, one hundred and fifty are female – but this does not stop them being capable of hunters and warriors.

The Ciirt strive to make the characters welcome, if unenthusiastically. Shelter (a patch of dry ground beneath a stinking awning of frayed hide, coated in Ciirt urine) is provided, along with the foul food the Ciirt adore. Everything the Ciirt do is directed by Maligaunt.

The settlement is divided into five yards.

Outer Yard

The ruined walls are low and crumbling, offering little in the way of protection, but as the Ciirt are the island's rulers and have no other enemies, they do not need protection from very much. Nevertheless, four warriors occupy the Outer Yard at most times just in case any stray monsters happen to wander towards the settlement. They are hardly vigilant: any Stealth rolls by an organised group of characters can be treated as one grade easier. The warriors are armed with simple flint weapons and if a fight is not going their way, they flee into the main compound.

Warriors' Yard

The warriors who have proved to be the strongest and best hunters and fighters get to live in this yard. They are served by the workers, take the better cuts from any hunt, and generally live more comfortable lives than the workers. Workers not meeting the warriors' standards or whims are beaten or butchered. Skulls, decapitated heads, amputated limbs, and other gruesome trophies are mounted in prominent positions as a constant reminder of the order of things. Occasionally the warriors fight among each other, usually to the death, and this helps keep numbers stable and maintain a pecking order.

Workers' Yard

Most Ciirt live here; males who want to be warriors, women, children, the old and the infirm. They huddle together in loose family groups, do what they are ordered to do by the warriors and the chief, eat what the warriors and chief leave them to eat, and live squalid, miserable lives. They have their own pecking order too, maintained through squabbles and fights of their own, often encouraged by the warriors. When food is scarce, the Ciirt workers turn on each other, eating the old and sick.

The yard is used as both homes and workshops. The workers make and repair flint and wooden weapons, make and repair clothes from hides and skins, and have a crude form of yarn that they spin into a rough cloth. It is always busy here, but always sombre.

Corrals

Although the Ciirt are hunters, they do keep and maintain a small stock of island goats and chickens for milk, eggs and occasionally meat. The chickens roam freely around the area, but have crude roosting boxes to nestle in overnight. The goats have their own corrals, and it is the job of the workers to milk the goats and collect the eggs every day. The milk is drunk raw, and also fermented into a foul-smelling kumis-style drink that the warriors adore. A separate store close to the corrals is used to make and house the kumis.

Chief's Yard

Ust is the chieftain of the Ciirt. He is the strongest warrior, having slaughtered his way into the position, just as every Ciirt chief has done for generations. He has the choice of the best wives, the best weapons, the best food, the best kumis. He orders the warriors and the workers, and acts as the High Priest of the tribe – the one who meets with Maligaunt and ensures Maligaunt's wishes are carried out.

His yard is less squalid than either the worker or warrior yards, and he has a an entire set of lean-tos that house his wives, children and his chosen warriors who act as his bodyguard. Ust's private lean-to is the circular area built against the wall that backs onto the Outer Yard and protected by a curved wall. In the remains of an old guard tower adjacent, his most prized wives are housed. His elite warriors are allowed to sleep with some of Urt's lesser wives, but no one can touch the prized wives who live in this special part of the compound.

Ust meets with Maligaunt whenever the demon decides to grace the Ciirt with his presence. Ust is in awe of the demon, and it is the rule that all Ciirt must fall to the floor and avert their eyes when Maligaunt walks among them. Only Ust is exempt; he must kneel, but can meet Maligaunt's gaze and, if permitted, walk with him. Ust has been shown various things in the tower and the caverns of the Walking Spells. This terrifying magic keeps Ust in check, because he has been told – as all Cirrt chieftains before him have been told – that on death he will ascend to a paradise where he rules thousands of Ciirt and has a harem of a thousand beautiful wives. If he fails to obey, then the machines will be his doom, and Maligaunt will allow the Walking Spells to wander freely around the settlement. Ust has seen what the spells can do, so he knows that the story of the paradise is also true. Ust obeys, and thus so do the Ciirt.

At the north-eastern corner of the settlement ruin is the only intact part of the Stronghold. Maligaunt's tower is where the demon resides, and he watches the arrival and welcoming of the characters for some time before making himself known. The tower is the only way to gain safe access to the caves below, and is guarded by four Ciirt warriors at all times, although they are rather inattentive unless being harried by Maligaunt. The tower, whilst habitable, possesses few comforts and is an untidy, smelly mess. Maligaunt occupies the middle floor, which once housed one of Loric Nygh's rooms and is where Maligaunt was first summoned.

Key to the Tower

Ground Floor

Tunnel

A double portcullis protects the entrance to the tower, which is gained through this short, low, tunnel. A winch mechanism still operates the rusted iron gates, although it is slow and ponderous to haul up and down the twin barriers. Each gate can be worked independently, or locked together so that both open with the same crank of the winch handle. The four Ciirt guards await intruders in the winch mechanism area. No one is allowed entry unless accompanied by Maligaunt. Intruders are repelled with force.

An Alarm spell has been cast on the threshold of the entrance into the tower proper, and it alerts Maligaunt to any intrusion immediately.

Kitchen

Unremarkable, and dominated by an ancient stone stove that has not been lit in centuries. At the location marked on the diagram is a heavy wooden trapdoor that opens onto the narrow, spiral stairs that lead into the caverns below the settlement. The trapdoor requires a combined STR of 26 to lift, plus a successful Brawn roll to lever against the centuries of accumulated dirt, grit, moss and so forth that effectively seals the door tightly shut. The steps are in good condition but slippery and uneven, and the stair shaft is not illuminated. The descent to the caverns is about 50 metres, and characters making the descent must succeed in an Athletics rolls to avoid slipping. Anyone that does slip tumbles 1d6 metres and sustains 1d6 damage as per the Falling rules in Mythras (page 78).

Storage Area

Again, unremarkable. It is packed with sacks of rotting grain and is the home of 100 ravenous rats that scatter when disturbed. Treat these as a SIZ 8 insect swarm (Mythras page 251), and they will bite to defend themselves.

First Floor

Four chambers are accessible from the landing.

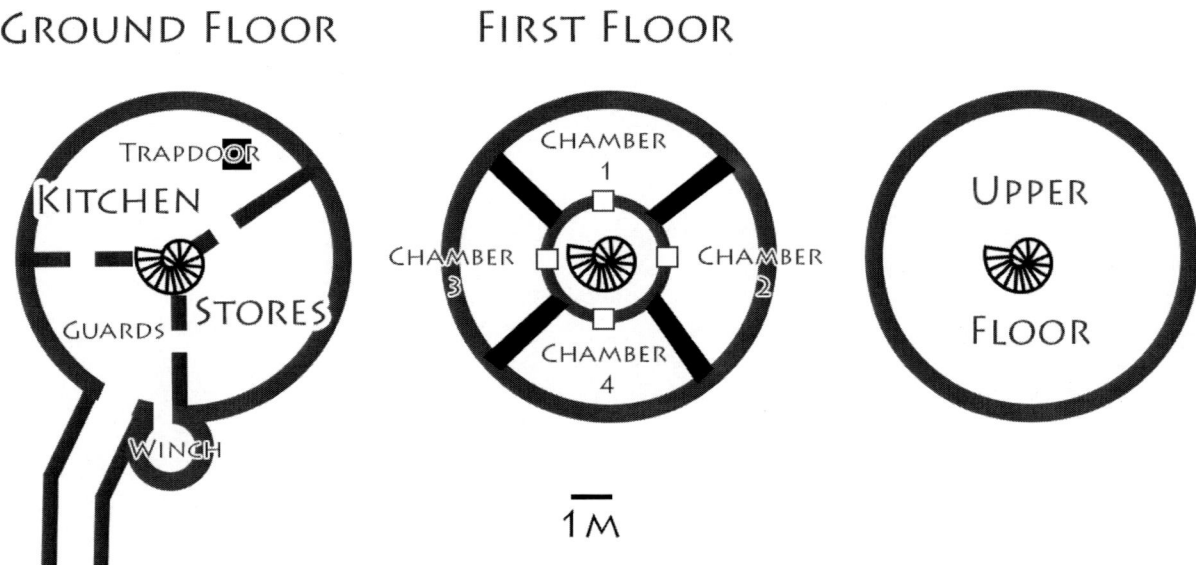

Chamber 1

Once this room belonged to Loric Nygh, and Maligaunt has attempted to keep it much as he left it. The large bed is fashioned into the jaws of a huge lizard, the tongue being a worn and soiled mattress of faded and stinking red satin, now decayed beyond use. Around the walls, draped from hooks, are a variety of robes Nygh himself wore and which Maligaunt now uses for ceremonial purposes with the Ciirt. The robes have been looked after by Maligaunt and, while hundreds of years old, are still in reasonable condition (although faded, tattered at the hem and somewhat smelly).

On the wall opposite the bed is a full-length tapestry depicting the sorcerer himself. Loric Nygh is a tall, handsome man with close cropped silver hair, a long moustache, and a sardonic grin. In one delicate hand he holds a skull, whilst in the other he holds a human heart. He wears one of the midnight-blue robes that now hangs in the room. Behind him, the tapestry depicts a vast battle between gigantic creatures that are indistinct and seem to writhe with their own life amongst the stitches of the tapestry. The tapestry is magical and provides a gateway to Loric Nygh's caverns below the Ciirt settlement. Concentrating on the tapestry for more than a few seconds causes the whole image to assume life-like focus and clarity. The figure of Loric Nygh smiles, steps to one side, and gestures for the watcher to approach. Stepping into the fabric transports the user directly into the caverns to the point marked Portal from Tower on the cavern complex diagram. The portal is two-way, and remains open until someone returns through it, stepping back into Chamber 1.

The entire experience of using this magical portal can be incredibly jarring. Anyone using it must make a successful Willpower roll or emerge psychically disturbed by the experience, with all skills reliant on INT and POW being one grade more difficult for 3d20 minutes.

Chamber 2

Maligaunt spends much of his time in this room, when not administering to the Ciirt. The door is locked and several complex and blasphemous runes have been scratched into its heavy black wood. The runes do not keep the door locked, and the mechanism can be picked without too much difficulty. However, the runes hold an Alarm spell and alert Maligaunt to any tampering with the door, meaning that the demon is aware of intruders when not in the room, or cannot be surprised if he is.

Inside the bedroom is a representation of the particular dimension Maligaunt calls home. Stepping into the room, one finds all notions of time and space gone. Instead one is in a cavern of seemingly infinite length and height, filled with a howling wind that brings random blasts of burning hot or freezing cold air. The room/cavern is filled with a soft, doleful music that, if listened to intently, turns out to be screams, very distant, extracted from their victims so as to produce a particular sound and pitch. Across the floor of the cavern, stretching away into the distance, are countless creatures resembling Maligaunt; tall, thin, extruded parodies of humans that are engaged in a multitude of domestic and menial tasks. Peering into the depths of the cavern it soon becomes possible to make-out the shape of a huge being, filling the cave from floor to ceiling, that is as bloated and corpulent as the demons are thin and emaciated. This Elder Being is constantly attended by the Maligaunt-like creatures, who scurry to feed and keep it clean. At the Elder Being's feet are the creatures who cannot work quickly enough and are being tortured to produce the mournful music that suffuses the cavern.

This hellish sight is but an illusion, created by Loric Nygh to taunt Maligaunt. The demon sought to escape its fate, but Loric Nygh found it amusing to produce the illusion in order to remind Maligaunt of his roots. Despite hating the contents of this room, Maligaunt is compelled to return to it. Only if Loric Nygh is restored to physical presence can the illusion be dispelled, and this is what Maligaunt craves more than anything.

Chamber 3

This chamber is packed, floor to ceiling, with the bones of dead Ciirt that Maligaunt has collected over the years, for reasons known only to himself. When the door is opened, the bones spill out with a horrible rattling sound.

Chamber 4

The door is firmly locked. Before she was transformed into a bronze statuette, Mistress Krystya spent a few nights here as Loric

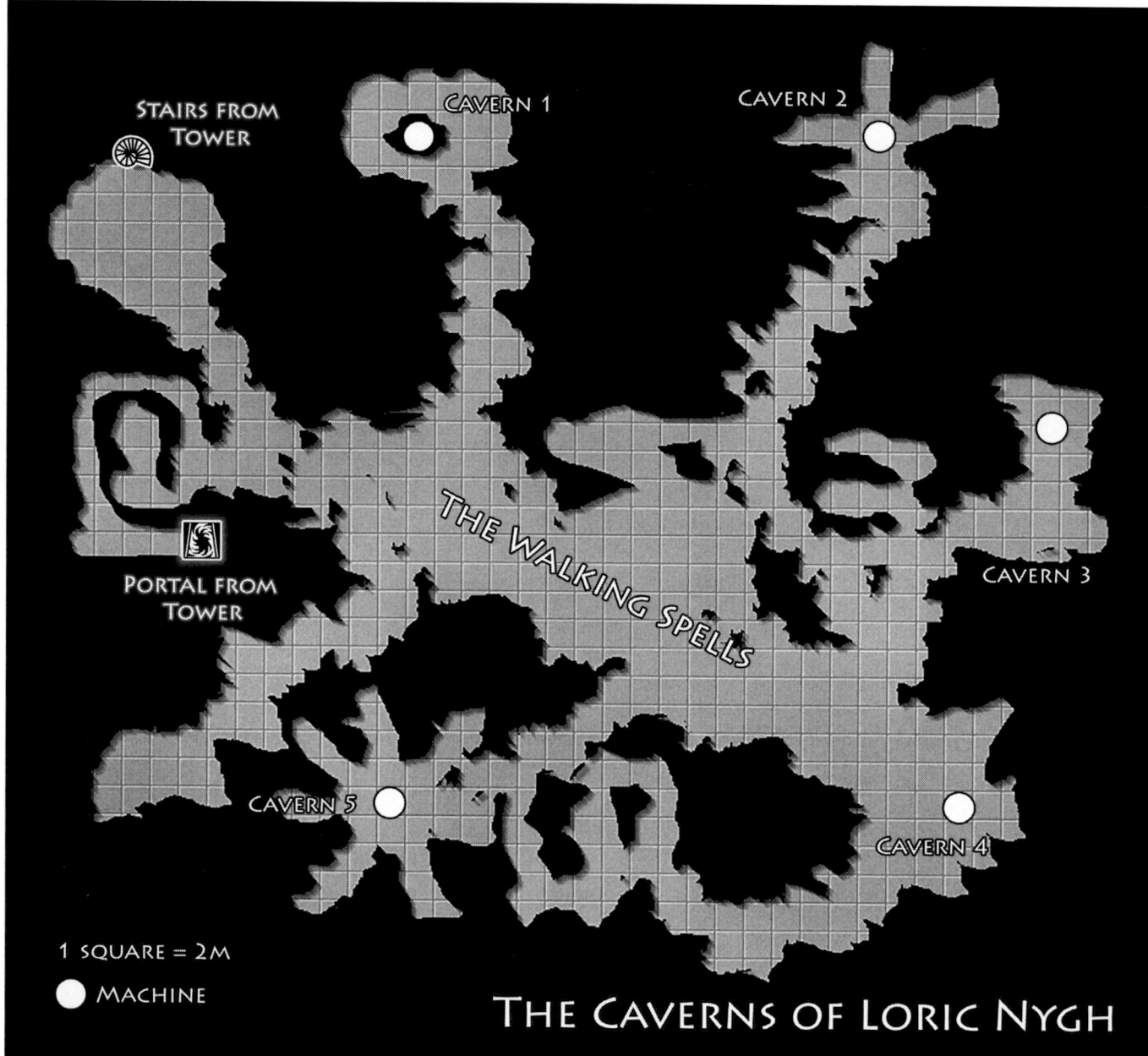

Nygh's prisoner. He treated her as a guest, and before he did what he did, they spent evenings in conversation. Nygh sketched her, and, after her transformation, painted her portrait; it still hangs on the wall, much faded and cracked, but most certainly the same woman represented in bronze. Her beauty is haunting, her clothes archaic. Behind her is a gleaming city of marble and red tile, some ancient place far away.

Anyone who is under the influence of the statuette who gazes upon the portrait must make a successful opposed roll of their Willpower against the Release the Lovers Passion; if the Passion wins the struggle, the character is instantly aware that they must find a way to the caverns deep below the tower to alleviate Krystya's suffering.

No one – not even Maligaunt – has set foot in this room since Loric Nygh placed the portrait there and locked it, a great deal of time ago.

Upper Floor

Utterly ruined and open to the elements, this was once a traditional sorcerer's laboratory. A variety of sorcerous runes are etched into the floor, while all around is the rubble and detritus of obscene experiments long-since abandoned (skulls, bones, twisted, unrecognisable things of flesh and atrophied matter).

The Caverns

About 50 metres directly below the Ciirt settlement are the natural caverns Loric Nygh purposed as his laboratory. Once the caverns reached the sea, but rockfalls have cut them off from a more extensive complex.

Maligaunt comes down here frequently, using the portal in Chamber 1 of the tower. He keeps torches made of reeds burning, so there is a frail illumination throughout the caverns, but many pockets of deep, flickering shadow. The walls are rough-hewn, the floor can be slippery in places, and the air is thick and humid

The open area of the cavern is where the Walking Spells reside. These are Loric Nygh's ultimate creations: sentient spells of remarkable power that can dominate and subjugate the wills of mortals. Loric Nygh built repulsive machines to manufacture these spells, and the same machines have sustained his soul since the Elder Beings imprisoned him.

The spells wander around the cavern complex aimlessly. Each branch from the main area of the complex has a 25% chance of a random spell wandering around it. Otherwise, the spells are always present in the marked area, wandering mindlessly. The spells appear as partially coherent figures, drifting several inches above the chasm floor, and never colliding. Because the light is poor, the pools of shadow easily conceal them, and deliberately spotting a wandering spell requires a Formidable Perception roll; however, once seen, others are spotted by standard Perception checks. Occasionally the spells fade from view, only to reappear metres away a few seconds later. The spells are silent, and this lends a sinister atmosphere to the caverns.

The Walking Spells

Each spell has been given a vaguely human resemblance, although they each retain some character that indicates the nature of their effect. The spells have no real intelligence, but they are aware of themselves and are driven by a desire to inhabit a physical form and thereby carry out their task – which is to be cast. The spells have two attributes; Willpower and Influence. Willpower is used in overpowering a physical host in an opposed roll. Influence is used by the spell to select its host. Anyone with an Insight skill equal to or less than the spell's Influence is a target for possession.

Once a spell has acquired a suitable host with its Influence, it attempts possession. The spell flows into the target via the nose and ears, adopting a silvery, watery nature which cannot be avoided or Evaded. Once absorbed by the target a Willpower struggle begins. The spell must overcome the target's Willpower in an opposed roll contest. If successful, it inhabits the target's soul. If unsuccessful, it is rejected and flows out of the target in the same way it entered. The target is left feeling drained and wasted and suffers a level of Fatigue.

If the target is overcome, the spell now resides within the soul and it cannot be extracted save through the powerful magics of Loric Nygh's Entropy Configurators. Its task now is to be cast as frequently as possible. The target still retains full control of his or her faculties, but is constantly aware of the nagging desire of the spell to be activated. These desires require a Willpower struggle for the spell to be supressed. The desires come to the fore under the following conditions:

- Whenever the individual desires to cast magic of any kind
- Whenever the individual is under physical, magical or mental threat, whether real or imagined
- If suffering a Serious or Major Wound
- If Magic Points fall below half their normal value
- If the individual decides to command the spell to cast.
- If the individual reaches a Fatigue level of Exhausted

For every time the spell is cast, the individual permanently loses 1d8 Magic Points which cannot be regenerated. Once Magic Points reach zero, the spell takes full control of the host and casts itself repeatedly, drawing on POW instead of Magic Points, until the host is dead (POW = zero or less). Then, the spell drifts from the host's remains and goes in search of another victim.

So the Walking Spells provide great power, but at a terrible cost, and the presence of the characters provides them with the means to achieve their underlying function.

Four Spells Shambling

Four spells are described below. Create others if you feel necessary.

Phenomena (Willpower 90%, Influence 70%)

Tall, thin and stooped, with a face dominated by a hawk-like nose and a forked beard braided into writhing tentacles.

This spell destroys natural elements. When cast, the spell spills forth from the caster and randomly attacks the dominant element within sight, replacing that element with its opposite. Therefore earth is transformed to water, air to fire and vice-versa. The casting is accompanied by a great roaring and the screeching sound of the element undergoing change.

The amount of the element transformed is equal in SIZ to the one tenth the spell's Influence: thus, 7 cubic metres of earth or rock; 7 cubic litres of water; 7 cubic metres of air and fire.

Note: since air is often the most prevalent element, air is only the targeted element if something else (stone, or fire, say) is not within immediate vision of the host.

Entropy Tango (Willpower 80%, Influence 75%)

A thick-set, dark-haired woman with an absence of facial features.

Entropy Tango blasts things into the whirling miasma of the multiverse. When cast, all things within a radius of 8 metres from the caster (but not the caster him or herself) simply vanish, leaving behind only a ghostly shadow which fades quickly. The affected things, whether living or inanimate, are hurled through the dimensions to arrive on a separate plane of existence instantaneously. No physical harm is done to those affected (although threats on the new plane might exist), but they must find their own way back to their original plane – which could prove extremely arduous or even impossible.

Mutability
(Willpower 75%, Influence 65%)

A tall, rather stern young woman possessing curiously round eyes, and a mouth that constantly changes its form – from mandibles to fangs, to a lamprey-like sucker, and so forth.

Mutability acts only on organic things. When cast, 1d8 Hit Points of the affected thing is transformed into a random substance permanently, although this does not automatically kill the target. Roll 1d20 for the Hit Location; any excess transformational damage affects the closest adjacent location. Roll 1d8 for the nature of the transformation:

1. Animal Limb
2. Arthropod Tentacle/appendage
3. Plant appendage
4. Inversion (the internal organs become externalised)
5. Bone
6. Metal (roll again: 1, Iron; 2, Bronze; 3, Lead; 4, Gold; 5, Silver; 6, Mercury)
7. Chaos Material (the affected things constantly changes and mutates, never retaining a fixed form for longer than a few seconds)
8. Caster's choice

Mutability does not kill. Even the head, after transformation, has intelligence and senses retained, although the appearance is now ghastly or disturbing beyond measure. The nature of the change is likely to induce incredible pain and may completely restrict movement (stone, bone or metal). The transformed part of the body is forever a part of that body and becomes an extensible part of the target, but with appropriate properties. Gamesmasters must judge exactly how such transformations afflict the target, and what the lasting effects will be.

Calling
(Willpower 65%, Influence 60%)

A short, corpulent male whose naked body is a webwork of superating scars and scabs. When cast, Calling summons-forth demonic or monstrous aid from a nearby dimension. Roll 1d8 for the nature of the summoning:

1. Giant Beetle
2. Chaos Hybrid
3. Ghoul
4. Harpy
5. SIZ 3d6+6 Insect Swarm
6. Manticore
7. Giant Octopus
8. 1d4 Skeletons
9. Winged Ape
10. Wyvern

The summoned creature can be commanded once by the caster, and remains in situ for 1d8 rounds, returning (if not slain) to its place of origin at the end.

The Caverns

Each of the caverns in this complex contains one of the Entropy Configurator machines Loric Nygh constructed during his physical life.

Cavern 1 – The Spell Focus

Examining the ceiling reveals that the entire rock is infused with throbbing veins carrying some kind of dark ichor. The rock is almost translucent, and just beneath the surface, pipes and other veins curve away into the stone. Any metal objects carried into this cavern crackle and burn with a brilliant blue energy, although these static trails are harmless (but warm to the touch). At the northern end of the cavern is the *Spell Focus* engine. This device allowed Loric Nygh to target and steal magic from other sorcerers and Elder Beings. The machine is a column of black, veined rock from which projects, at head-height, a hollow dome of crystal. Placing one's head into the crystal allows the user to perceive the web-like structure of the higher dimensions: a million silver threads, like the branches of a tree, that lead to cloudy, indistinct realms of existence. Simply by focusing on a branch and the realm it leads to allows the user to view the substance of that realm in terms of the magical energy it contains. Only Loric Nygh can make proper use of the device, since only he knows the incantations required to navigate the dimensions. However, by targeting a realm, he can pinpoint individual sorcerers resident there and plunder their magic, mentally conveying the nature of the magic into the Focus device to be recalled at a later point. This process usually kills the unfortunate sorcerer at the other end, but preserves the substance of the theft, allowing Loric Nygh to use it at his discretion.

Cavern 2 – The Forge

High ceilinged, this dark, damp cavern contains the device used by Loric Nygh to create the statuettes Sool so cruelly desired. At one end of the cavern, supported by golden statues depicting grotesque creatures of hell, is a huge globe of translucent material, half-filled with a restless, roiling, golden liquid. Access to the innards of the globe is provided by a funnel-like affair at the top of the machine.

Living bodies are dumped into the Forge, which immediately sets to work, separating the soul from the flesh and casting it into a bronze statuette that is vomited unceremoniously from the mouth of one of the demons supporting the globe. The flesh is dissolved by the vile, golden liquid. The whole casting process takes around an hour, while the unfortunate being worked by the Forge screams in torment. All goes silent when the statuette is spat from the leering mouth of the demon.

The Forge cannot end of the torment of Mistress Krystya or her lover: another engine is required to do that. But in proximity to the engineer of their torment, the souls captured in the statuette cry out in terror at the memory of what they endured during the process of their imprisonment.

Cavern 3 – The Sculptor

This cavern contains a pyramidal structure of bones and sinew. This is the Sculptor – a machine capable of reversing the process of the Forge in Cavern 2. It can take a damned soul and sculpt for it a new physical form. If the Sool Statuette is placed in the gaping maw of bones at the base of the machine, it sets to its grim work. The bones of the device begin to move, knitting together the sinew surrounding the machine to build a new body and inject the offered soul.

What only Loric Nygh knows is that the Sculptor plays one, nasty trick. The body it fashions is one of the Maggots of Torment (see page 7), which are ejected from the Sculptor's maw as a sickly, writhing, hideous and pitiful creature that is doomed to eternal misery if not killed. If cast into the Sculptor, this is the fate of the souls of Mistress Krystya and Lord Sleane: freed from a bronze prison, and cast into individual prisons of flesh. The products of the Sculptor can, however, be slain by one decent sword-blow, and the two lovers scream for this release after the Sculptor has done its work. Only in this way can their curse be broken.

Cavern 4 – Machine of the Walking Spells

The machine that creates living spells resembles a malformed maggot, the size of a small ship. It is suspended from the ceiling of the cavern by sinuous strands of some dark material and writhes sickeningly at the approach of the characters. The Walking Spells at large in the chasm converge around the yawning maw of the maggot and await their potential new companion. New living spells can be created by Loric Nygh, if he has been restored to physical presence, using complex magics. The maggot, after several hours of pained effort, vomits a new spell of immense power from its ooze-dripping mouth, to either wander the chasm complex or take charge of a new soul.

Destroying this hideous engine prevents new Walking Spells from being created, but has no effect on the existing ones.

Cavern 5 – Loric Nygh's Soul Chamber

A single engine dominates this cavern. A semi-transparent tube that stretches the height of the cavern, supported by more golden statues of demons and things of hell. Within the tube is a dark, formless, almost smoke-like substance: the soul of Loric Nygh. Lying at the feet of one of the demons is a pile of shattered, semi-fossilised bones – all that remains of the sorcerer's body.

Loric Nygh created this device to imprison certain souls he wanted to torment or learn from. When the Elder Beings came to scourge his stronghold, they used the machine to imprison it's own creator. Loric Nygh's broken body was thrown before this device and his soul fed into it. The Elder Beings considered that eternal imprisonment within the machine was a fitting and apt punishment for this upstart mortal.

So it is that Loric Nygh has been here for more centuries than he can remember, tended by Maligaunt, and waiting for the day when a suitable host would appear.

One of the tactics Maligaunt uses is to promise to reveal the secret to freeing Mistress Krystya from her statue, if someone volunteers to step into the cage to test the effectiveness of this machine. "It enhances the soul," Maligaunt says. "And it can bring great magical power." He is not lying, but neither is this the full story.

The machine has a cage, held between the outstretched hands of one of the supporting statues. If a character has been captured, or has volunteered for the transformation, he or she is placed in this cage. Immediately the darkness held within the tube coalesces and flows into the cage, penetrating and eventually engulfing the imprisoned victim. After several minutes, the darkness fades and the character physically remains, unharmed, outwardly, but inside, the character is no more. The body is now home to Loric Nygh, and the sorcerer desires revenge.

Kindly Games Masters may permit the victim a resistance against this most hostile of takeovers. Loric Nygh engages in Spirit Combat with the victim, using his Spectral Possession 77% (1d8 Spirit Damage) to target the victim's Magic Points. The victim can resist with either Binding (if an animist) or a Formidable Willpower roll. Nygh's soul has 21 Magic Points and if defeated retreats sullenly to the main chamber, unable to affect that victim again (but perfectly able to attack another potential host).

If successful, Loric Nygh does not reveal his true nature immediately, and affects disorientation for an hour or so while he gets to grips with his new physical form. When speaking he uses the victim's old voice, although he can, when he wishes, use his own, booming, sardonic tones. Only after dumping the Sool Statuette into the Sculptor, and witnessing the cruel release, does he howl with insane laughter and declare his restored nature. He cares little for the surviving characters; but he would like to see the Walking Spells given new homes, and he commands Maligaunt (who is weeping tears of happiness at the return of his master) to convey the characters to Cavern 4 so they might be rewarded with more power than they could ever know. Ciirt guards assist in this process if the characters decide to decline Loric Nygh's kind offer. They can fight their way free (conduct a melee with the Ciirt to decide this) or comply. If they comply, then the Walking Spells attempt to infect suitable hosts. If successful, again, the characters can leave Nygh's Stronghold, but are now victims of Loric Nygh's cruelty. If the Walking Spells reject the offered hosts, then the characters have had a very narrow escape with their lives and souls intact.

Ending the Scenario

There are many possible endings to Madness and Other Colours. Here are some suggestions.

Loric Nygh Restored

Nygh begins his plot for revenge on his destroyers. Using the Focus he begins to assemble magics for use against the Elder Beings. This might take years, but Loric Nygh, able to roam the dimensions once again, is a very real threat indeed. Perhaps the remaining characters decide to pledge allegiance to him and assist in his revenge. Perhaps they decide to bring his tyranny to a final end.

The Statuette Destroyed

The Sculptor can end the entombed soul's torment, but at the price of another, unless the fleshy prisons it fashions are destroyed. This, at least, allows the souls of Mistress Krystya and Lord Sleane to depart to whatever afterlife fate has in store for them. Freeing the souls breaks the curse afflicting either Baldomeer, Serjedny or the characters – whoever has charge of the statuette.

The Characters Possessed

Either by a Walking Spell and/or Loric Nygh. The characters infected by spells are free to leave, but the Walking Spells are with them always, and seek to cause their own havoc at every available opportunity, as described earlier in the scenario. Even if Loric Nygh is destroyed, the characters have no known way of ridding themselves of the Spells – although who knows, a sorcerer may exist, somewhere in the world, who can free them from this bind?

The Characters Flee

Fleeing Nygh's Stronghold without ending the entombed souls' torment is no escape. Madness afflicts whoever possesses the statuette, or last possessed it, and that person is forever cursed with their own torment: complete the task by returning to Nygh's Stronghold, or succumb to an insanity that will, eventually, lead to their own death.

If, however, the characters somehow manage to dispose of the statue, and evade Loric Nygh and Maligaunt's plans, they will have been a party to an adventure that could have led to the return of one of the most vile sorcerers ever spawned. Who knows? They may have knowledge, and a desire, to return to Nygh's Stronghold and put-paid to the sorcerer and his infernal machines once and for all. The Elder Beings themselves might even be willing to assist in such an enterprise. But that, as they say, is another story…

Non-Player Character Statistics

Serjedny The Immaculate

Serjedny resembles a somewhat pained weasel. His thinning hair accentuates the length and narrowness of his nose, and his thin, reedy mouth is often twisted into a sneering grin. He has the annoying habit of cracking his knuckles, especially when excited by something, and his wealthy clothes hang ill-fittingly from his lanky frame. Serjedny can be either ingratiatingly polite or downright rude, depending on the social standing of the company. His full hatred and disdain, however, is reserved for his old rival, Baldomeer The Vain.

Serjedny	Attributes
STR: 9	Action Points: 3
CON: 9	Damage Modifier: -1d2
SIZ: 9	Magic Points: 17
DEX: 13	Movement: 6 metres
INT: 17	Initiative Bonus: 15
POW: 17	Armour: None
CHA: 14	Magic: Folk Magic

Skills: Art Appreciation 99%, Athletics 25%, Brawn 24%, Commerce 90%, Conceal 31%, Dance 30%, Deceit 58%, Endurance 31%, Evade 39%, First Aid 38%, Influence 55%, Insight 60%, Locale 80%, Lore (Art History) 85%, Perception 59%, Ride 30%, Sing 41%, Stealth 70%, Streetwise 37%, Swim 36%, Willpower 51%

Passions: Hate Baldomeer 85%, Covet Artworks 90%, Vain 85%

Magic
Folk Magic 78% (Appraise, Clean, Perfume)

1d20	Location	AP/HP
1–3	Right Leg	0/4
4–6	Left Leg	0/4
7–9	Abdomen	0/5
10–12	Chest	0/6
13–15	Right Arm	0/3
16–18	Left Arm	0/3
19–20	Head	0/4

Combat Style: Foppish Slashery (Dagger) 60%

Weapon	Size/Force	Reach	Damage	AP/HP
Dagger	S	S	1d4+1-1d2	6/8

Baldomeer The Vain

Moon-faced and moon-bellied, Baldomeer The Vain has an open, charming disposition with many a wry joke or scathing witticism to hand if required. He wears his hair in oiled ringlets, has a perfectly waxed beard, and carries a bejewelled looking glass at his sash belt so he can constantly admire himself. Baldomeer dislikes Serjedny intensely, but views his rival as a nuisance more than a threat. Making a find he knows Serjedny wants amuses him, but he does not go out of his way to provoke the man. Such little provocations seem to happen quite by accident.

Baldomeer	Attributes
STR: 13	Action Points: 3
CON: 9	Damage Modifier: 0
SIZ: 10	Magic Points: 11
DEX: 12	Movement: 6 metres
INT: 16	Initiative Bonus: 14
POW: 11	Armour: None
CHA: 15	Magic: None

Skills: Art Appreciation 104%, Athletics 31%, Brawn 39%, Commerce 90%, Conceal 70%, Dance 41%, Deceit 84%, Endurance 40%, Evade 33%, First Aid 55%, Influence 42%, Insight 45%, Locale 88%, Lore (Art History) 95%, Perception 63%, Ride 40%, Sing 44%, Stealth 32%, Streetwise 53%, Swim 33%, Willpower 38%

Passions: Hate Serjedny 78%, Release the Lovers 80%, Covet Artworks 85%

1d20	Location	AP/HP
1–3	Right Leg	0/4
4–6	Left Leg	0/4
7–9	Abdomen	0/5
10–12	Chest	0/6
13–15	Right Arm	0/3
16–18	Left Arm	0/3
19–20	Head	0/4

Combat Style: Art Critic Self Defence (Dagger) 34%

Weapon	Size/Force	Reach	Damage	AP/HP
Dagger	S	S	1d4+1	6/8

Maligaunt

Maligaunt is of a race of demons dedicated to serve a master's specific needs and they are compelled to preserve the summoner's life if it is threatened. They can adopt many forms and, in this manifestation Maligaunt is extremely tall and rake-thin. His almost hairless skull is dome-like and pitted with acne. His long-fingered hands terminate in sharp claws that the demon uses to defend himself, or force others to do his bidding. He dresses in the discarded robes of his master, and is always accompanied by the stench of mold.

Maligaunt is utterly loyal to Loric Nygh, even though he is loathe to make the admission. His entire being is dedicated to returning his master to physical form and Maligaunt is quite capable of scheming to achieve this end. Trapped here for so long with the Ciirt, he has come to thoroughly despise them. For a while he tried to educate them, but their limited intellects resisted all forms of education. So instead, he turned to dominating and manipulating them. His various folk magic spells are used to torment and reward the Ciirt as he sees fit, and over the many centuries he has become their god. The Ciirt avert their eyes when Maligaunt passes among them, unless he ululates a command to gaze upon him. They fear him of course, but do his bidding. On a command from the demon the Ciirt will turn against the characters en-masse without a second thought.

Maligaunt	Attributes
STR: 17	Action Points: 3
CON: 17	Damage Modifier: +1d6
SIZ: 19	Magic Points: 16
DEX: 21	Movement: 7 metres
INT: 14	Initiative Bonus: 18
POW: 16	Armour: None
CHA: 8	Magic: Folk Magic

Skills: Athletics 71%, Brawn 65%, Conceal 44%, Dance 63%, Deceit 90%, Endurance 65%, Evade 83%, First Aid 25%, Influence 61%, Insight 75%, Locale 90%, Lore (Loric Nygh) 95%, Perception 73%, Ride 37%, Sing 24%, Stealth 52%, Survival 90%, Swim 34%, Willpower 84%

Passions: Loyalty to Loric Nygh 100%, Despise Ciirt 85%

Folk Magic 90% (Alarm, Avert, Demoralise, Fanaticism, Repugnance)

1d20	Location	AP/HP
1–3	Right Leg	0/8
4–6	Left Leg	0/8
7–9	Abdomen	0/9
10–12	Chest	0/10
13–15	Right Arm	0/7
16–18	Left Arm	0/7
19–20	Head	0/8

Combat Style: Demonic Talons (Claws) 84%

Maligaunt's claws are strong enough and long enough to Impale.

Weapon	Size/Force	Reach	Damage	AP/HP
Claws	M	T	1d4+1d6	1/7

Ciirt

Short, hunched, and covered in thick, wiry hair. Their foreheads slope sharply and are thick-browed, their noses flattened globes of skin with wide, sensitive nostrils. Their arms are disproportionately long and their legs stocky and short. They can move surprisingly quickly in an ape-like manner.

The Ciirt are a degenerate species hailing originally from lands far from here, where they were occasionally food for giants and other predators. A century or so ago, they left (how is not clear) and found themselves on the periphery of Nygh's Stronghold, where they have lived ever since. They possess only a basic intelligence, with little reasoning power, and are easily impressed by displays of finery and minor magic. They are able hunters, and have managed to eke a living from the land, but readily resort to cannibalism when times are hard.

They view Maligaunt as a God. They worship him as he worships Loric Nygh. They follow his bidding, although are easily cowed if faced with superior numbers and/or skill.

Quite brutal when fighting, Ciirt have no concept of mercy – only ways of supplementing the food chain.

The statistics here are for typical Ciirt warriors. Workers have only Unarmed at 30%. Ust has the same statistics as a Ciirt warrior, but treat all skills as 10 percentiles higher and his Combat Style as 84%.

Typical Ciirt	Attributes
STR: 11	Action Points: 2
CON: 14	Damage Modifier: None
SIZ: 11	Magic Points: 11
DEX: 11	Movement: 6 metres
INT: 6	Initiative Bonus: 9
POW: 11	Armour: Thick skin and wiry hair
CHA: 7	Magic: None

Skills: Athletics 52%, Brawn 42%, Deceit 57%, Endurance 48%, Evade 62%, Perception 61%, Unarmed 52%, Willpower 42%

Passions: Fear and Obey Maligaunt 90%, Eat Things 85%

1d20	Location	AP/HP
1–3	Right Leg	1/5
4–6	Left Leg	1/5
7–9	Abdomen	1/6
10–12	Chest	1/7
13–15	Right Arm	1/4
16–18	Left Arm	1/4
19–20	Head	1/5

Combat Style: Ciirt Hunter (Spear, Sling) 62%

Weapon	Size/Force	Reach	Damage	AP/HP
Shortspear	M	L	1d8+1	4/5
Sling	L	-	1d8	1/2

Loric Nygh – Discorporated Sorceror

Loric Nygh is the epitome of the evil, twisted sorcerer: clever, cunning, ambitious, cruel, and ultimately brought down by his own folly. Having spent close to 2,000 years as a disembodied soul in a jar, he is, naturally, utterly insane and bent on revenge. He intends to have it, using his engines and other means to punish the Elder Beings who imprisoned him. All life is expendable; no one has any value beyond the part they play in his dastardly plans.

If an adventurer becomes host to Loric Nygh's vile soul, it is *not* recommended that the sorcerer become a player-character. His evil knows no bounds, and his powers are too immense for mortal players to handle; instead, have Loric Nygh remain a major Non-Player Character, and representing a new enemy for the party to battle against in future campaigns.

Physical attributes are not applicable to Loric Nygh in his soul-form. Once he occupies a human body, he takes on those physical attributes. INT and POW become those provided below. All skills relying in STR, CON, SIZ and DEX are those of the victim. Other skills are noted in his statistics.

Spells: Loric Nygh knows most of the Sorcery spells provided in the Mythras rules (indeed, he invented several of them) and more besides. Provide him with just about any sorcerous ability you care to think of.

Loric Nygh	Attributes
INT: 18	Action Points: 3
POW: 21	Spirit Damage: 1d8
CHA: 14	Magic Points: 21
	Initiative Bonus: 16
	Abilities: Discorporate, Manifestation, Miasma

Skills: Deceit 90%, Influence 81%, Insight 85%, Invocation 99%, Lore (Demons) 95%, Perception 69%, Shaping 99%, Willpower 102%

Passions: Disdain Everyone 100%, Rule the World 99%

Island Encounters

Giant Beetle

Beetle, Giant	Attributes	
STR: 19	Action Points	2
CON: 17	Damage Modifier	+1d6
SIZ: 19	Magic Points	4
DEX: 13	Movement	12m
INS: 9	Initiative Bonus	11
POW: 4	Armour	Chitin
	Abilities	Burrowing, Formidable Natural Weapons

1d20	Location	AP/HP
1	Right Rear Leg	5/7
2	Left Rear Leg	5/7
3	Right Middle Leg	5/7
4	Left Middle Leg	5/7
5-9	Abdomen	5/9
10-13	Thorax	5/10
14	Right Front Leg	5/7
15	Left Front Leg	5/7
16-20	Head	5/8

Skills

Athletics 62%, Brawn 68%, Endurance 74%, Evade 26%, Perception 53%, Willpower 38%

Combat Style & Weapons

Beetle Bite (Mandibles) 72%

Weapon	Size/Force	Reach	Damage	AP/HP
Mandibles	M	T	1d6+1d6	As for Head

BASILISK

Basilisk		Attributes	
STR: 5		Action Points	2
CON: 11		Damage Modifier	-1d6
SIZ: 5		Magic Points	19
DEX: 13		Movement	6m
INS: 11		Initiative Bonus	12
POW: 16		Armour	Scales
		Abilities	Gaze Attack, Life Sense, Terrifying

1d20	Location	AP/HP
1-3	Tail	1/4
4-5	Right Hind Leg	1/4
6-7	Left Hind Leg	1/4
8-10	Hindquarters	1/5
11-14	Forequarters	1/6
15-16	Right Winglet	1/3
17-18	Left Winglet	1/3
19-20	Head	1/4

Skills

Athletics 48%, Brawn 30%, Endurance 52%, Evade 66%, Perception 69%, Willpower 78%

Combat Style & Weapons

Gaze Attack (see Mythras page 229)

GIANT MANTIS

Mantis, Giant		Attributes	
STR: 13		Action Points	3
CON: 13		Damage Modifier	+1d4
SIZ: 19		Magic Points	4
DEX: 25		Movement	6m, 10m (Flying)
INS: 9		Initiative Bonus	17
POW: 4		Armour	Chitin
		Abilities	Camouflaged, Flying, Grappler

1d20	Location	AP/HP
1	Right Rear Leg	3/6
2	Left Rear Leg	3/6
3-4	Metathorax	3/8
5	Mid Right Leg	3/6
6	Mid Left Leg	3/6
7-10	Prothorax	3/9
11-12	Right Wing	3/6
13-14	Left Wing	3/6
15-16	Right Forelimb	3/6
17-18	Left Forelimb	3/6
19-20	Head	3/7

Skills

Athletics 78%, Brawn 72%, Endurance 56%, Evade 80%, Fly 68%, Perception 53%, Stealth 74%, Willpower 48%

Combat Style & Weapons

Unseen Death (Scything Limbs, Bite) 78%

Weapon	Size/Force	Reach	Damage	AP/HP
Forelimb	L	VL	1d6+1d4	As for Limb
Mandibles	M	M	1d4+1d4	As for Head